DISCIPLES: JESUS WITH US

by

Rev. Riley Richardson
with
Henry Neufeld

Energion Publications
P. O. Box 841
Gonzalez, FL 32560
http://www.energionpubs.com
pubs@energion.com

Energion Publications
P. O. Box 841
Gonzalez, FL 32560

This book includes material previously published as pamphlets in the
Participatory Study Series from Energion Publications, including *I
Want to Pray, God's Good News for You, You Were Made for Worship,
Repentance and Rejoicing,* and *What About Fasting?*

Cover Design and Layout by Jason Neufeld, jasonneufelddesign.com.

ISBN: 1-893729-49-4

PREFACE

This is a simple book. That's what it's intended to be.

If you're reading this book we assume you have recently decided to become a Christian, or perhaps you have decided to renew your commitment and don't know how to go about it.

We're not going to bore you with advanced theology. We will tell you about some terms that you're going to hear around church and what they mean.

When you became a Christian, you didn't come to a destination, you started on a journey. That journey will continue through the rest of your life.

Follow the simple guidelines in this book to get off to a good start on that journey.

There are going to be lots of things to *do* in this book. You may be wondering about that. "Didn't I hear somewhere that salvation is a gift? Why are there all these things to *do*?" you may ask.

Your salvation is a gift, and you have it. But if you were given a brand new car as a gift, and then left it to sit in your driveway, what would be the benefit of that gift? What if you drove it, but never checked the maintenance schedule?

Salvation is a gift. Now you're going to learn how to enjoy it and make the most of it.

IV

CONTACT INFORMATION

TABLE OF CONTENTS

WHAT HAVE I DONE?

You've become a Christian. There are many different words that might have been used. You're saved. You joined the church. You became part of the body of Christ. Every group has it's vocabulary. What does it all mean?

Let's review how you got here.

Paul writes in his letter to the Romans that:

> "All of us have sinned and fallen short of God's glory." (Romans 3:23).

This doesn't say that:

- God has rejected everyone.
- God doesn't like them.

It does say that we, as human beings, have fallen short of the wonderful purpose and plan that God has for you. You might have been at rock bottom when you decided to accept Jesus. You might have just been impressed with his teachings and decided that you could do better than you were.

Here are some of the things the Bible says about human beings:

- We are created to be like God (Genesis 1:26)
- We were given control over the earth (Genesis 1:28)
- We were made a little lower than God (Psalm 8:5)
- We have fallen short of this wonderful goal of emulating God's character and of using our full capabilities.

God hasn't separated Himself from us, we have separated ourselves from God. (See Luke 15:11-32)

Jesus stepped into this inadequacy. Here's what Jesus did:

- He brought to us understanding of God's character. (Hebrews 1:3)
- He carried the burden of our sins (1 Peter 2:24)
- He gave us a way to live right (1 Peter 2:24)
- He opened the way to God (Hebrews 4:14-16)

Jesus has shown us the glorious purpose God has for us and how we can attain it.

> *God's Son has all the brightness of God's own glory and is like him in every way. (Hebrews 1:3)*

A LIFE OF SURRENDER

The idea of surrendering control of one's life to someone else is very frightening to some. But what is it that God is actually asking of us? Think of someone standing by a high cliff. There is a choice to be free of the laws of nature and jump, or to accept them and take proper care. To choose life by surrender is not to give up anything good. One simply accepts the physical laws that exist and by which the universe runs. Accept them and live; reject them and die. It is the same thing with Christ's moral laws: accept and live or reject and die.

> *Today I am giving you a choice. You can choose life and success or death and disaster. (Deuteronomy 30:15)*

The choice between life and death, the opportunity, and even the ultimate result—our entry into heaven, is assured by the free gift God gave in Jesus. Some people stop right there. But to do that is to miss out on some of the excitement, fulfillment, joy, and peace that Jesus has for those who will follow him.

Jesus said that the most important commandment of the law was: "Love the Lord your God with all your heart, soul, and mind. . . . The second most important commandment is like this one. And it is, 'Love others as much as you love yourself.'"

The Bible also teaches that we must put this love into action (1 John 4:20,21).

> *Children, you show love for others by truly helping them, and not merely by talking about it. (1 John 3:18)*

You may be wondering about heaven and hell. It's likely that you thought about these things. Taking the option of going to heaven rather than hell was the focus. For many people the point of Christianity or any religion is to assure one's place in another world, to make sure you go to heaven. That's good! But there is much more to following

Jesus than that. Jesus showed as a good way of life here and now! The Bible tells us about an eternal reward and eternal punishment, but what it tells us most about is following Jesus in this world.

By following Jesus in this life we are preparing to be in His presence for eternity. (See John 14:1-3)

This is all about action. Do you also need to believe specific things and learn specific things about God in order to be saved? You may be wondering if this is something like school, with passing and failing grades.

No, you haven't landed in that type of program. Jesus grades on the "grace curve" that makes it possible for everyone to be a success.

When Jesus was asked a question about this very topic he responded by using an illustration about a shepherd separating sheep from goats. He said of the ones who would be accepted into the kingdom: "Whenever you did it for any of my people, no matter how unimportant they seemed, you did it for me" (Matthew 25:31-46). Jesus is asking you to love others, and to continue to grow in love.

You won't be perfect, and neither will all the Christians around you be perfect. In fact, we will all be considerably less than perfect together. But that's part of the plan as we learn and grow together.

Repentance

Because we are all so imperfect, we need repentance. Repentance means "turning away," "changing one's mind," or "going in a different direction." If we find we are going the wrong direction, we will not be able to get where we are going no matter how fast we go. In fact, we might be considered foolish for not slowing down. If we want to accomplish our goals we need to be unafraid of acknowledging when we are going in the wrong direction. This is why Ezekiel tells the Israelites that God doesn't want anyone to die. "I enjoy seeing them turn from their sins and live" (Ezekiel 33:11-12). And this is followed with a promise: "And remind them that when wicked people stop sinning, their past sins will be completely forgiven, and they won't be punished."

Christians need to live in an attitude of repentance. "What's that?" you may ask.

It's a bit like this. When you're driving down the road and you're not sure if you're going in the right direction, or if you're on the right road, what do you do? You look for road signs. When you see one, you check and see if you're going the right direction. If you find you're on the wrong road, you turn around and find the right road. If you find you're already on the right road, you keep right on going.

Living the Christian life is much like that. An attitude of repentance means that we constantly check the road signs of life to see if we're going in the right direction. Then we make corrections as needed.

You don't have to be an especially astonishingly bad sinner to repent. You simply need to realize you have further to go, and you need to correct your course.

JUSTIFICATION AND SANCTIFICATION

Both justification and sanctification are God's gifts resulting from the life, death and resurrection of Jesus.

What is justification?

God promises that when we repent, or turn to the right path he will accept us, we will be right with him (1 John 1:9). This is what many Christians call being saved.

What is sanctification?

Sanctification is the work of God's grace in our lives helping us to become victorious over habitual sin. God loves and accepts us just as we are, but God loves us too much to leave us the way we are. Through sanctification God works in our lives to help us overcome sin and temptations. God's ultimate goal in our lives is to make us more like His Son Jesus. The work of Sanctification is a life long journey as you grow in your relationship with God.

Then, because you belong to Christ Jesus, God will bless you with peace that no one can completely understand. And this peace will control the way you think and feel. (Philippians 4:7)

What should I do?

1. Pray and accept the message God has sent you through Jesus.
2. Determine to turn from the things that keep you away from God's full purpose for your life.
3. Find a group of Christians who believe in living the love of Jesus on a daily basis and join with them for worship and action.
4. Look for ways to make your world better.
5. Read your Bible, listening for the voice of God as you do.

You know God's laws, and it isn't impossible to obey them. . . . Today I'm giving you a choice. You can choose life and success or death and disaster. . . . On the other hand, you might choose to disobey the LORD and reject him. So I'm warning you that if you bow down and worship other gods, you won't have long to live. (Deuteronomy 30:11-18 selected)

SALVATION PRAYER

Dear Father in Heaven,

I admit that I have sinned and fallen short of Your glorious purpose for me.

I acknowledge Jesus as Your Son and my Lord and Savior. I accept the message of love You sent through Him.

I turn from my sins and ask to be brought back to Your plan for me.

I surrender my life to You.

I ask You to fill me with Your Spirit so that I can live a Christ-like life.

In Jesus' name,

Amen

ACTIONS AND DISCUSSION

1. Would you say you are "laid back" or do you like to feel control and follow a plan?

2. What are the top three priorities in your life?

   a. _____

   b. _____

   c. _____

3. Take the next 10 minutes and just think about:

   a) things that you are thankful for

   b) concerns

   c) your relationship with God; what's good and what do you think could be better?

RESOURCES:

Participatory Study Series Tracts: *God's Good News for You, What is the Good News?**

---

* Participatory Study Series, from http://www.participatorystudyseries.com.

Stott, John R. R. <u>Basic Christianity</u>. Grand Rapids, MI:
Wm B. Eerdman's Publishing Company, 1981.

PRAYER

We start with prayer, because prayer is the way in which we communicate with God, and thus should be central to your Christian life. It will combine with other activities, such as Bible study and spending time simply listening, but prayer will always be a key.

WHAT IS PRAYER?

Prayer is a conversation with God.

- Prayer should be simple (Matthew 6:7)
- Prayer can be private (Matthew 6:6)
- Prayer can be public (Acts 7:59, 60)
- Prayer can include both your needs and those of others (Matthew 6:9-13; James 1:5; 1 John 5:16)
- Prayer comes from our love for God and for one another (1 John 4:7,20)

- Prayer can happen whether I feel "good" enough or not (Luke 18:9 14)!

You should pray like this:
Our Father in heaven,
Help us to honor your name.
Come and set up your kingdom,
So that everyone on earth will obey you, as you are obeyed
in heaven.
Give us our food for today.
Forgive us for doing wrong,
As we forgive others.
Keep us from being tempted
And protect us from evil.
--Matthew 6:9-13

HOW DO I GO ABOUT PRAYING?

Prayer begins with us realizing that we want to talk to our Father in heaven.

Some basic principles to remember as you pray:

1. Ask and you will receive. (Matthew 7:7)
2. Our heavenly father may keep wrong things from us for our own good (James 4:1-10).
3. God wants to hear us (Isaiah 65:23-24).
4. God wants us to hear Him (Isaiah 66:4).

WHAT IF I CAN'T THINK OF ANYTHING TO SAY?

1. Read your Bible and think about what you read.
2. Find quiet time.
3. Listen for God to speak to you.

4. Try printed prayers, such as the Lord's prayer (Matthew 6:9-13) or the prayer of Jesus in John 17.
5. Don't be afraid to say what's in your heart-even questions.

PRAYER ATTITUDE

The only "prescription" for prayer is that we DO pray. Even devout Christians come to points in their lives where they feel inadequate and ineffective in prayer. The Apostle Paul clearly understood this, and so writes in Romans 8:26, "And in the same way the Spirit helps us in our weakness, for we do not know how to prayer as we should. . . ."

Paul assures us here that God understands us and knows our every need—even in the area of prayer.

Frequently Christians wait to pray until they can talk politely to God. Remember that God already knows what you are feeling and thinking. You can go ahead and talk about it.

Many prayers recorded in the Bible, including the Psalms were offered in anger or despair (Psalm 22, 1 Kings 19:3-5). God wants you to converse with him and learn and grow. Prayer is not so much about getting things as it is about learning and growing.

ANSWERS

Will your prayers be answered? There are many types of answers. Practice spending time listening when you pray.

Listen to those around you. But also look for God's answer to your prayers.

Remember that you are talking with your heavenly Father and that He wants what is best for you. He always hears, but He is not always going to do what you say in the time limit you demand. Prayer isn't like a vending machine. It is a discipline that you practice so you can grow.

One good practice is to keep a prayer journal. In this journal you will record your requests and your answers. If you do this, don't forget to also record anything you hear from the Lord during your prayer time.

PRAYER IS FOR ANYONE

Some Christians are afraid to pray because they don't feel that they are important enough. But God is our heavenly Father and we are all his children. Anyone can pray. You don't have to be a special person or be good enough. God will hear and wants to hear from you, his child.

ACTIONS AND DISCUSSION

1. Try keeping a prayer journal for the next four weeks. Include prayers of:

   Worries/concerns and needs
   Thanksgiving and celebrations
   Yourself

   Make sure you leave room for the answers.

RESOURCES:

Participatory Study Series Tracts: *Prayer Scriptures for Prayer Warriors, Self Defense for Prayer Warriors, So You're an Intercessor!**

Dalton, Perry and Henry E. Neufeld. <u>I Want to Pray!</u> Gonzalez, FL: Energion Publications, 2006. Basic guide to prayer.

Neufeld, Myrtle. <u>Directed Paths</u>. Gonzalez, FL: Energion Publications, 2005. Stories of answered prayer and God's guidance.

Yancey, Philip. <u>Prayer: Does it Make Any Difference?</u> Grand Rapids, MI: Zondervan, 2006.

---

* Participatory Study Series, from http:// www.participatorystudyseries.com.

Prayer Journal Page

Date	Prayer or Answer

Joining with Others

Finding a Church Congregation

If you talked with someone about your decision to follow Jesus, and they invited you to their church, then that is a good place to start. If that wasn't the scenario, you need to find a group of Christians to join. It is very difficult, if not impossible, to be a Christian by yourself. You need the company and support of other believers.

Here are the key things you need to find in a church fellowship:

- Friendly and supportive members
  You need to feel welcome. The church needs to be a place where you can grow, and where you are not afraid to be yourself.

- Accountability
  Though you want a church that is friendly and supportive, your church is a sort of extended family. You need your brothers and sisters in the church to

hold you accountable. This means helping you to keep on track as you follow Jesus. There is a balance between the first point (welcoming) and this one. It's very easy for a church that has strong accountability to become nagging and judgmental. Look for the balance that works for you.

- A place to study and learn
Small groups, Sunday School classes, preaching that involves you and helps you learn, and other church educational programs help you and your family to grow in knowledge.

- A place to worship
Worship can involve different things for different people. If you are a person who has never been in church, you may feel a bit strange. If you haven't been to church in many years, and are just returning, you may find that many things have changed. Look for worship that is comfortable for you, but that gets you involved.

- A place to serve
We'll talk about service later. Look for a church that is involved in serving the community so you can get on board and help that happen. If the church isn't active, you're going to have a hard time finding a place to use your God-given skills in service.

ACTIONS AND DISCUSSION

1. What do you look for in a fellowship of believers?

    a. _____

    b. _____

    c. _____

    d. _____

    e. _____

2. Prioritize these five characteristics, 1-5.

RESOURCES:

Neufeld, Jody. <u>52 Weeks of Ordinary People – Extraordinary God.</u> Gonzalez, FL: Energion Publications, 2005. Short devotional studies for small groups.

BIBLE STUDY

One of the keys to developing your Christian life will be Bible reading and study. You need to plan a regular pattern of Bible study, even if you just start with a few minutes each day.

Try to get involved in a Sunday School class at church so that you can get a better idea how to study the Bible, or look for a small group of other Christians who are studying the Bible and ask to join them. Because the Bible was written to many different people at many different times, it is not always simple to find God's will for you as you study.

GETTING MORE FROM YOUR BIBLE READING[*]

There is no shortcut in Bible study. If you want to find what God has for you in scripture you will have to dig. There are some things you can do to make your study time more profitable. In this chapter we outline a simple approach to Bible study which can help you both with devotional reading and with deeper study.

As you become more and more experienced, more things will become clear to you. The following are some suggestions for reading the Bible for yourself:

PREPARATION

Gather Materials - have pen, paper, highlighters or other markers and all materials you will need for study available.

Conditions - Find a place and time you can study. If you study well with music playing, put some on. If you prefer quiet, arrange for a quiet place. If you are a morning person, get up 30 minutes earlier. If you are a night person, turn off the TV and spend the evening with God.

Resources - Get a small, well-selected set of study materials. Your resources may change as God leads you on your discipleship journey.

---

* These suggestions are taken from the pamphlet *I Want to Study the Bible*, part of the Participatory Bible Study method published by Energion Publications. For more information, see www.deepbiblestudy.com.

PRAYER

Pray specifically for an open mind to understand, an open heart to receive, and enabling grace for the actions you will need to take.

Claim these promises:

> *But if we confess our sins to God, he can always be trusted to forgive us and take our sins away. (1 John 1:9)*

> *I will sprinkle you with clean water, and you will be clean and acceptable to me. I will wash away everything that makes you unclean, and I will remove your disgusting idols. I will take away your stubborn heart and give you a new heart and a desire to be faithful. You will have only pure thoughts, because I will put my Spirit in you and make you eager to obey my laws and teachings. (Ezekiel 36:25-27)*

GET AN OVERVIEW OF THE PASSAGE

Read the passage multiple times. Twelve or more can be a real blessing, but any number from 3 times up will help. Memorizing is useful, at least of key texts. (This will also require you to select key texts.) Reading from a Bible version different from your usual one helps you with your concentration and opens up different ways of understanding the passage.

At this point don't use commentaries, study notes, your concordance, anything which takes your concentration from the passage you are studying.

STUDY THE BACKGROUND

Find out who wrote the passage, to whom it was written, what is the situation being addressed, and what type of literature it is. Study Bibles generally have this information at the beginning of each book or a Bible handbook can be helpful.

The following chart may help you with possible types of literature:

Type	Examples
Poem	Song of Songs, Psalm 78, 104, 119
Song/Hymn	Song of Miriam (Exodus 15:1-18), Song of Deborah (Judges 5), Psalm 19, 27
Story	Ruth, Esther
History	1 & 2 Samuel, 1 & 2 Kings, 1 & 2 Chronicles, Nehemiah, Ezra
Parable	Luke 16
Allegory	Ezekiel 16
Doctrinal teaching	Matthew 5-7
Wisdom Literature	Proverbs, (this may overlap with Poems)
Prophetic Oracle	Isaiah 14:1-23

Vision report	Ezekiel 1,Daniel 7, 8
Prayer	Psalm 12, Daniel 9

MEDITATE, QUESTION, RESEARCH, COMPARE (REPEAT AS NEEDED)

Meditate on the passage. If you are having difficulty meditating, think about telling someone else about the passage, such as a friend in need of encouragement, someone who is unsaved, or a child. Consider: What questions might they ask about this passage? You can formulate thought questions or fact questions. Fact questions are about what the author is actually saying. Thought questions may lead you to other revelations well beyond the intended statement of the passage.

You can use outlining at this stage, comparison to other scriptures, to writers in church history, or to current experience. Ask: What similar experience are we having today? Can this help me understand the passage? For example, if you have had a vision will that might help you understand Ezekiel's vision in Ezekiel 1. Ask your friends about experiences they have had.

Some historical writers you might consult include Jerome, Aquinas, Augustine, Martin Luther, John Wesley, John Calvin, Charles Spurgeon and many, many others.

Share your Thoughts

Ask yourself how the scripture has applied in your experience. Get to know the person you are sharing with. Share your experience and then the text. Always work from your own personal experience with God.

Store up the experiences your friends share with you to use in studying other scripture.

Example Passage

1 Kings 19:11-18

1. Begin your study with prayer.

2. Read the passage several times. Can you tell this story in your own words?

3. Read 1 Kings 17-19.

4. Check a Bible Handbook or study Bible for the background of 1 Kings.

5. Consider how Elijah feels through this experience. Consider what God is trying to accomplish by giving Elijah these experiences.

6. How did Elijah know the Lord was not in the wind, the earthquake or the fire?

7. Can the Lord appear in such violent events? (Use your concordance, looking up wind, fire, and earthquake.)

8. Does God respond to Elijah's complaint? (Only indirectly; he gives him a task.)

9. Is Elijah as much alone as he feels he is? (No, there are 7,000 more faithful people, v. 18.)

10.What other Bible characters have experienced something similar to this? (Daniel 3-the fiery furnace.)

11.What people in church history may have experienced something similar to this? (Any martyr or person who has suffered persecution.)

12.Have you experienced similar feelings?

13.Have you ever felt completely alone in your faith?

14.Share your experiences!!

Example Prayer for Bible Study

Lord, take from me any thought habits which will keep me from hearing. Make me open to your voice and your voice alone.

Lord, help me to accept your people as my brothers and sisters in your kingdom. Let me learn and grow from both their weaknesses and their strengths.

Lord, I trust you to reveal yourself to your people the way you know is best. Let your will be done.

Lord, let me not only recognize but obey your voice. Let my actions be conformed to your will. Help me to love my neighbor as myself.

In Jesus' name, Amen.

Resources

Bible(s)[1]

- For quick reading (overview):
  Contemporary English Version (CEV)
  The Message
  New Living Translation (NLT)

---

1 If you are interested in the question of why there are many translations and how they came about, Energion Publications also publishes a book *What's in a Version?* with guidance on how Bible versions are produced and how to choose one for your needs.

- For study or reading:
  New International Version (NIV)
  Revised English Bible (REB)
- For study:
  New Revised Standard Version (NRSV)
  (This list is not exhaustive.)

BIBLE DICTIONARIES

HarperCollins Bible Dictionary

New International Bible Dictionary

CONCORDANCES

The NIV Exhaustive Concordance.

BIBLES WITH STUDY NOTES

Oxford Study Bible (REB)

New Oxford Annotated Bible (NRSV)

Spirit Filled Life Bible

The NIV Study Bible (Zondervan)

The Learning Bible (CEV)

Bible Atlases

Many study Bibles include good Bible atlases, but a separate Bible Atlas or world history atlas can be useful.

Oxford Bible Atlas

The Harper Atlas of World History

Bible Handbooks

The Cambridge Companion to the Bible

Zondervan Handbook to the Bible

ACTIONS AND DISCUSSION

1. Find a small Bible study group or a Sunday School class.

2. Begin to study your Bible daily.

3. Where will you study?

4. When will you study?

5. Make a plan and a commitment to Bible study.

RESOURCES:

Participatory Study Series Tracts, *I Want to Study the Bible, Bible Study Tools.*[*]

Moore, Beth. Believing God. Nashville: B&H Publishing Group, 2004.

Neufeld, Henry. Participating in the Bible. Gonzalez, FL: Energion Publications, forthcoming, June 2007. An expanded guide based on this chapter.

Fee, Gordon and Douglas Stuart. How to Read the Bible for All Its Worth, 3rd Revised Edition. Grand Rapids, MI: Zondervan, 2003. A more advance Bible study manual.

---

* Participatory Study Series, from http://www.participatorystudyseries.com.

Warren, Rick. <u>Rick Warren's Bible Study Methods: Twelve Ways You Can Unlock God's Word</u>. Grand Rapids, MI: Zondervan, 2006.

<u>The Participatory Study Method</u>, http://www.deepbiblestudy.net. Various articles on Bible study.

SERVICE

Yes, it's true. We're going to put you to work. But that's only because we care about you and want you to develop into a mature, joyful follower of Jesus, and that path will only come through service to others.

One of the things we suggested you look for as you searched for a church home was a place where you could be of service. Now you may be thinking that areas of service involve mostly preaching, visiting the sick, counseling people in trouble, or some other task that requires some skill.

If you have those skills, that may be precisely what you're going to do. If you're a businessman who talks to other businessmen on a regular basis, you may find your way easily into teaching Sunday School or even occasionally preaching. Those things will depend on the needs of the church you attend. You may also find that you need to teach the same thing in the church as you did in the secular world.

But if your skills are different, shall we say a little less obvious, there is still a place for you in the church, and that place is just as important.

You may be needed to greet people at the door and give them a friendly welcome. Someone may need to help direct cars in the parking lot. Every church needs to be cleaned and repaired from time to time. No matter what it is that you do, you're going to find that there is a need for that skill in your church and in your community.

And don't just think of the things you can do in the church. You may already be doing service. Have you already been helping your neighbors? That's service. Do you give money and time to community projects? That's also service.

As you become a disciple, you want to join your efforts to help others with those of your church family so that you can all be more effective in showing Jesus to the world.

ACTIONS AND DISCUSSION

1. Find out who in your church coordinates volunteer service and find out how to volunteer for service in your church.

2. Make an appointment with your pastor or the volunteer coordinator of your church. Bring a short list of your interests and gifts. Get involved!

RESOURCES:

Participatory Study Series Tracts: *Spiritual Gifts* series.[*]

Neufeld, Henry. <u>Identifying Your Gifts and Service, Small Group Edition</u>. Gonzalez, FL: Energion Publications, 2007. A Holy Spirit led process for discovering your gifts and where to use them in service.

---

[*] Participatory Study Series, from http:// www.participatorystudyseries.com..

GIFTS

You just knew we were going to talk about money sooner or later, didn't you? Well, here we are. Often we cloud this issue by talking about our gifts in combination with our time, the gift of friendship, or other things. It makes it easier to talk about.

But you might as well know right now that it takes money to run a church. It takes money to provide service to others. The issue is how we are going to use the money.

The keyword that you are going to hear is "tithing." A tithe is 10% of your income. Christians will proudly announce that they are tithers, meaning that they regularly give that 10% to their local church.

Now is not the time to settle all the detailed issues about tithing. You're going to hear debates about whether tithing is a New Testament law, whether tithe should be paid on your earnings before or after taxes, and whether you can give your tithe to whatever ministry you like or if it should all be given to your local church. Let all those arguments fly right by you. Don't let them land and take up you're time.

At the same time you may be thinking, "Ten percent! Nobody told me it was going to cost me this much! Maybe I made a mistake!"

Here's a suggestion for how to deal with money. Make your resources a subject of prayer. Simply ask God what you should give as a start, then continue to ask him what you should give as you move forward. Pray about it regularly.

Consider giving regularly, no matter what amount you start with. You might start with 1% of your income. That would be $10.00 out of a thousand. On the other hand, you might start by putting a dollar in the offering plate every week. Just take your ideas to God in prayer. Be ready to adjust your giving as you feel led.

Remember that God has promised to be faithful to you if you are faithful.

> [10] *I am the* LORD *All-Powerful, and I challenge you to put me to the test. Bring the entire ten percent into the storehouse, so there will be food in my house. Then I will open the windows of heaven and flood you with blessing after blessing. -- Malachi 3:10*

ACTIONS AND DISCUSSION

1. Take a step of faith and give the tithe <u>God</u> wants you to give.

2. Add a note regarding this tithe in your prayer journal and pray about it regularly.

RESOURCES:

Nowery, Kirk. <u>The Stewardship of Life</u>. Camarillo, CA: Spire Resources, 2004.

Moving Onward

The previous chapters of this little book have led you through a number of the basics of living life as a Christian. In this chapter let's look forward to some of the additional things you can do to keep growing into a better and better relationship with Jesus.

Worship

The Best Way to Worship

Since Cain and Abel first made their offering of thanks to God, we, His children, have been trying to get our worship of God 'right'. This story of Cain and Abel tells us that the worship that pleases God is worship that comes from a humble, thankful heart. Worship is not a responsibility or obligation; it is an opportunity for me to express love to my Lord who loved me first!

WORSHIPERS IN THE BIBLE

David - Credited with writing most of the psalms, King David is said to have been a man after God's heart (1 Samuel 13:14). His worship reflects the depth of his relationship with his Lord - joy, tears, dancing (2 Samuel 6:14), and song.

Moses and Miriam - In Exodus 15 this brother and sister wrote a beautiful song of praise to God who brought them out of Egypt. The Israelites danced to this song following their deliverance.

Mary - Luke (2) records the beautiful words of Jesus' mother as she worships with her cousin, Elizabeth, praising God for the miracles in their lives

Anna - it is said (Luke 2) that she was a prophetess and never left the temple but worshiped day and night

King Jehoshaphat's army- this has to be one of the great acts of worship and steps of faith in Biblical history! It truly gives us a true example of how to 'wage war in the heavenlies' (2 Chronicles 20)! Take some time right now to read this.

The Last Supper - Christ's creation of the sacrament of communion shows us how reconciliation is a key element in the worship of our Lord.

WORSHIP IS MORE THAN MUSIC

Music for many people is a perfect vehicle to express the words of their heart to God. Whether it is with vocal singing or dance or using instruments, music with all its styles can bring us into an 'intimate conversation' with God.

Reading and sharing Scripture can be just as intimate as we express God's inspired words back to Him. The making of banners, paintings, sculpture, and video design are all ways that allow us to use the gifts God gives us to worship him.

Giving of our tithes and offerings is a wonderful way to express our thanksgiving and faith to our God who is faithful and extravagant!

Any time members of the Body come together with the intent to glorify God is an opportunity to worship Him. It could even happen in our dining room! The ideal is that everything we do becomes an act of worship.

ORDERLY WORSHIP

Order doesn't always mean quiet, controlled, and solemn. A baseball game has an order to it, but many variations can occur as the game is played, all within this order. Those who love baseball may find the kind of order displayed in a hockey game disturbing, yet there is an order specified by the rules and traditions of the game.

In a church service, the unity of those who gather and their purpose make up the "rules of the game" that set the tone and the boundaries of the service. Within that unity, the worship service can take many different and unique forms, and still be orderly.

But just as the rules and implements used in one game are part of a system, so are the rules of worship. A player on ice skates would be out of place in a baseball game, while a baseball bat-quite useful in its place-would probably be used as a weapon in a hockey game.

When we visit another church or are involved in worship, we need to be aware of how others are worshiping, so that we can act in unity with that worship. We need to give up our own desires in order to worship with others. But just as I can choose to watch one sport and not another, so I can choose to worship where I can express myself to God. It is the heart that counts.

FINDING PRAISE AND WORSHIP MUSIC

There are many, many books and CDs available.

Cried Holy, by Floyd Ellsworth, available from Doxology Records (CD).

A Touch of Glory: It's Your Destiny, by Lindell Cooley (Book).

Faithful Friend (CD), by Leah Taylor.

There are many more available. Here are some good sources:

Integrity Music, www.integritymusic.com.

Vineyard Music (USA) www.vmg.com/usa/

iPod users can find a whole section of Christian music at iTunes. These are also available for your PC.

FASTING

"Is not this the kind of fasting I have chosen: to loose the chains of injustice and untie the cords of the yoke, to set the oppressed free and break every yoke? Is it not to share your food with the hungry and to provide the poor wanderer with shelter- when you see the naked, to clothe him, and not to turn away from your own flesh and blood?" - Isaiah 58:6-7

WHAT IS FASTING?

In the Bible fasting refers to restricting one's diet, including refraining from eating and drinking entirely. As Isaiah says in the text quoted above, fasting can include other activities that are done for God.

In modern times, fasting has been extended to include giving up other activities that are part of one's routine, generally things that one enjoys.

Some types of fasts include not eating for one or more meals, not eating and drinking for a short period of time (always consider your health), leaving off certain types of entertainment (an evening with the TV turned off, and limiting your diet such as not eating sweets, or drinking soft drinks. These are only a few examples.

The Purpose of Fasting

You already have God's attention-God doesn't have any trouble keeping up with what people are doing. But fasting does have to do with helping us get closer to God, mostly by focusing our attention on God.

The fast that God chooses, as discussed in Isaiah 58, has to do with treating other people appropriately and carrying out God's mission. If we are not right with God, fasting is not going to persuade Him to do things He would not otherwise do.

What fasting can do is help us focus on God and bring ourselves more into tune with what God wants us to do.

In a fast, when you think of the thing you have given up, it should be a remainder to focus your attention on God and to listen for God's will. Sometimes God's will might be for you to quit fasting, and take some form of action.

Fasting, Prayer, and Action

In prayer we tell God how we are feeling and thinking and what we want. Prayer, in the sense of speaking to God, should include time for listening to God's will. Fasting is especially useful in focusing us on God's will and on how we can come closer to God's plan for us. The primary impact of fasting is on our listening to what the Holy Spirit wants to communicate to us.

Do not fast if there is a question of health. If you want to find something to help you focus on God find something that you can leave off that does not threaten your health. Cooperate with your physician. If you have questions about the wisdom of fasting, consult your physician and also your pastor or someone who helps keep you accountable.

Here are some examples of some types of fasts.

- Limiting entertainment or reading
  Limiting movies, television viewing, music, or the type of books that one reads can help focus your mind on spiritual things.
- One or two meals
  This is the most common type of fast. Some people will fast a single meal in a day, or fast from the morning until some time in the afternoon or evening. This can be done either a single time, or regularly on a particular day of the week.
- All food for a period of time
  Leaving off all food for a specific period of time. Be certain that your health is good enough for this type of fast. (Any food fast should be considered carefully.)
- All food and drink for a period of time
  While this kind of fast, usually for a day or so, can be very useful, it is also the most dangerous, because the human body cannot function without water for very long.
- Limited food and drink
  Again, this fast is done for a period of time. Ezekiel went on an extended fast of this type. If we

understand the measures correctly, however, Ezekiel was miraculously sustained through his fast.

The key to the best type of fast is to discover what helps you focus on God. That is the best fast for you.

Tell the leaders and people to come together at the temple. Order them to go without eating and to pray sincerely. - Joel 1:14

When you Miss the Mark

But if we confess our sins to God, he can always be trusted to forgive us and take our sins away. - 1 John 1:9

Psalm 51 provides an example of repentance.

1. Acknowledge - verse 3

I know about my sins, and I cannot forget my terrible guilt.

Completely admit to what you have done wrong, without excuses.

2. Cleanse - verse 7

Wash me with hyssop until I am clean and whiter than snow.

Ask God to cleanse you and make you whole.

3. RESTORE - VERSE 12

Make me as happy as you did when you saved me; make me want to obey!

Ask to be restored to God's favor.

4. TEACH - VERSE 13

I will teach sinners your Law, and they will return to you.

You teach others by sharing your testimony about what God has done in your life.

5. PRAISE GOD - VERSE 15

Help me to speak, and I will praise you, Lord.

Praise God for what He has done. This has the additional effect of reminding you of what He has done and keeping you humble before Him.

6. WORSHIP - VERSES 18, 19

Then you will be pleased with the proper sacrifices, and we will offer bulls on your altar once again.

Worship is the natural consequence of a relationship with God.

IF YOU STILL FEEL GUILTY

There are several ways in which repentance can fail.

- Making excuses instead of fully acknowledging guilt

See the story of Saul in 1 Samuel 15, especially verses 20 and 21. Instead of acknowledging his guilt, he denies it and adds an excuse. Contrast David's action in 2 Samuel 11.

David vs. Saul

2 Samuel 11-12	1 Samuel 13-15
Murder and Adultery	Disobedience
Prophet sent	Prophet sent
Admits guilt	Denies guilt and makes excuses
Accepts punishment as just	Complains about punishment
Is accepted by God	Is rejected by God

Before I confessed my sins, my bones felt limp, and I groaned all day long. . . . So I confessed my sins and told them all to you. . . . Then you forgave me and took away my guilt. – Psalm 32:3-5

- Not fully changing your mind about your actions

To repent means to change your mind. If you are not determined to change, you have not really repented.

- No desire for cleansing

Forgiveness is followed by cleansing. If we don't want the cleansing, we won't receive the forgiveness.

- Refusing joy

Sometimes being sorrowful makes us feel important, so we refuse the joy of restoration.

Repentance puts us back in line with the heavenly attitude. Refusing joy takes us back off the heavenly attitude.

> *Jesus said, "In the same way there is more happiness in heaven because of one sinner who turns to God than over ninety-nine good people who don't need to."*
> *- Luke 15:7*

- Unworthiness

Feeling that you cannot possibly be cleansed or be fit for God's kingdom. But God has made us fit for his kingdom.

> *All of this shows that God judges fairly and that he is making you fit to share in his kingdom for which you are suffering. — 2 Thessalonians 1:5*

- Unbelief

Either you don't believe that God can forgive you or will forgive you. (See 1 John 1:9)

> *If you forgive others for the wrongs they do to you, your Father in heaven will forgive you. But if you don't forgive others, your Father will not forgive your sins. — Matthew 6:14, 15*

- Unforgiveness

Unforgiveness includes holding onto our resentments and grudges. We can fail to forgive because we have been hurt too much. We can also fail to forgive because we refuse to admit that we have been hurt.

> *You know that you have been taught, "An eye for an eye and a tooth for a tooth." But I tell you not to try to get even with a person who has done something to you." –* *Matthew 5:38, 39a*

THE UNPARDONABLE SIN?

One of the tasks of the Holy Spirit is to convict of sin. If we turn away the Holy Spirit so much that we no longer hear His voice telling us that "this is a sin" or "this is wrong," we will no longer ask for pardon and it will, in fact, be too late.

TRUSTING GOD FOR THE RESULTS

One of the rewards of an ongoing relationship with God is a trust in what God is doing. When we trust God for the final result, we can have peace and joy even in trouble. (Romans 5:3-5)

> *We gladly suffer, because we know that suffering helps us to endure. And endurance builds character, which gives us a hope that will never disappoint us. – Romans 5:3b-5a*

SHARING YOUR FAITH

As you learn more about Christianity, you will want to share the experience and the joy that you have found. But you can get started on that right now by sharing your testimony. A testimony is simply your story. It's good to think about this in advance. Your first Christian testimony is about how you decided to follow Jesus in the first place.

It consists of three elements:

1. What was your situation?

2. How you encountered Jesus

3. The result.

We can chart it like this:

Your Testimony	
I was . . .	What brought you to the point of looking for something new, something special in your life? This doesn't have to be a story of complete disaster; it can simply be that you were looking for something more. Be honest about your past and what you were looking for.
Encounter with Jesus	How did it happen? Were you introduced by a friend? Did you find information in a book? Was it a time of personal prayer?
I am . . .	Who are you now? Stick with your own story, because that is what you know. Don't try for special "spiritual" language.

Now when you are asked, you can respond quickly and with confidence.

ACTIONS AND DISCUSSION

1. Prepare your own testimony.

Your Testimony	
I was . . .	
Encounter with Jesus	
I am . . .	

2. Share your testimony with other believers as practice.

GLOSSARY

Confession – saying the same thing as God does about your sins, freely acknowledging that you have done wrong and that you are responsible.

Deacon – this church office varies by churches, but generally refers to those who do service to other people in and for the church.

Elder – this church office varies in different churches, but usually refers to the core leadership of a church.

Fasting – most commonly going without food or on a limited diet for a period of time as an aid to meditation, prayer, and spiritual discipline. Sometimes extended to mean going without other desirable activities such as television or secular reading.

Justification – being brought into a good relationship with God. This is accomplished because of the death of Jesus on the cross.

Pastor – usually the central leader of a church, responsible for general direction, preaching, counseling members, and some administration.

Prayer – conversation with God, whether undertaken individually or in a group. Preferably includes listening to God and meditating.

Repentance – changing one's course of action, turning around.

Salvation – refers to coming into right relationship with God, living as his child, and eventually living eternally with him in heaven.

Sanctification – the process of becoming closer and closer to God and more like his goal for us.

Tithe – 10% of one's income given for God's work through the church. In Biblical times the tithe was given to the tabernacle or temple for God's service.

APPENDIX A: USING PRAYER SCRIPTURES

*For our struggle is not against enemies of blood and flesh,
but against the rulers, against the authorities, against the
cosmic powers of this present darkness, against the
spiritual forces of evil in the heavenly places.
- Ephesians 6:12*

GUIDELINES FOR PRAYERS

- Pray each prayer for each person or group on your list.
- Use the scripture prayers in addition to, not instead of your personal prayers to God.
- Include praise and thanks in all your prayers.
- While praying scriptural prayers mention specific people, events or groups.
- Use your name or see a loved one in these scriptural prayers.
- Pray for your church, prayer group, pastor, study group, family and friends with each of these prayers.
- Find others to pray with you and for you.

- Leave time to listen to what God has to say to you.

For Truth and Blessing

Father, I thank You for *_____'s faith in the Lord Jesus and his love for all the saints. I will not stop giving thanks for him and praying for him. I ask in the name of Jesus, glorious Father, that You give him a spirit of wisdom and of revelation and a deep knowledge of You.

I pray that the eyes of his understanding be filled with light so he will know the hope of his calling, the richness of his glorious inheritance among the saints. I pray that he may know just how immeasurably great Your power is for those who have faith. I pray, Father, that he will recognize how effectively Your power works, just the way it did when You raised Christ from the dead.

I praise You, Father, that Jesus now sits at Your right hand in heavenly places, Father, above every power and authority and force of power and lordship and everyone's fame that can be mentioned not only in this world but in the world to come. All things have been subjected under the feet of Jesus, and He has become the head of his body, the church in all matters. He fills the universe everywhere!
- adapted from Ephesians 1:15-23

*fill in a name from your prayer list for each blank line or italicized pronoun.

That Each will Stand Firm

With the powerful grace of God in mind I kneel before You, Father. You are the One from Whom every family in heaven and on the earth gets its name. All fame belongs to You. I ask, Father, that You give _____ the power to reach into the inner man by the Spirit. I ask that Christ will dwell in his understanding through faith. I ask that with all the saints he be rooted deeply and grounded firmly in love, and be able to grasp just how wide and long and high and deep Your love is. May he know it, even though it is too great to really understand, so he may be filled with Your fullness.

Father, I give You the glory. May You receive praise from generation to generation forever, because You are the One Who works among us so powerfully that You are able to do more than we can ask or even imagine.
- adapted from Ephesians 3:14-21

For God's Armor

Father, I ask that _____'s strength come from being in Your mighty grasp. I ask that he be equipped with all Your armor, God, so that he can stand firm against the devil's schemes. I know, Lord, that we are not fighting against people, but rather against authorities, rulers in the darkness of this world, and against highly placed evil spiritual forces. So I pray that he put on all the armor that You provide. Then he will be able to stand firm when that evil day comes. I pray that he be able to stand all the way through the battle.

May he Stand ready!

Belt of Truth

Wrap truth around his waist as a belt

Breastplate of Righteousness

Let God's righteousness fully protect his torso as a breastplate

Shoes of Peace

May he be prepared with God's good news of peace

Shield of Faith

May he take up faith as a shield

Helmet of Salvation

Wrap God's salvation around his head like a helmet

Sword of the Spirit

And let him take up God's word as a sword.

Father, I lift up before You now prayers and petitions continually in the Spirit. [This is a good time to pray in the Spirit.] I intercede for _____ and petition You for him. I pray that he may have the right message to speak when he opens his mouth, to make known boldly the mystery of the gospel, even in chains. Let him be as bold as he ought to.
- adapted from Ephesians 6:10-20

For Protection

Lord, I live in Your hiding place, and I stay under Your shelter. Lord, You are my fortress and my refuge. I place my trust in You.

Lord, I ask that You keep me safe from hidden traps and deadly diseases. Spread Your wings over me so that I can find security. May your truth and faithfulness be my shield and defense.

I praise You Lord, that I don't need to worry about night terrors, nor about arrows flying during the day. I don't have to fear plagues striking in the darkness or sudden disaster at noon. Even though a thousand fall at my right side, or even ten thousand, I will be completely safe. I will see their destruction, but I won't be touched by it.

That's because You, Lord, are my place of refuge. You, Lord Most High are my fortress. No disaster will strike me anywhere, nor will I be wounded at home.

Father God, command your angels to guard me wherever I go. Let them grab me and lift me to safety if I stumble. In Your strength Lord, I can tread on lions young and old; on deadly serpents and adders.

The Lord responds:

"Because you cling to me, I will rescue you. Because you acknowledge my reputation, I will lift you high above your trouble.

"Call Me, and I will answer you. I will be with you in trouble. I will deliver you and show you honor. I will satisfy you fully with long life, and you will see My salvation."
- adapted from Psalm 91

I lift up my eyes to the hills-
from where will my help come?
My help comes from the LORD,
who made heaven and earth.
He will not let your foot be moved;
he who keeps you will not slumber.
He who keeps Israel
will neither slumber nor sleep.

The LORD is your keeper;
the LORD is your shade
at your right hand.
The sun shall not strike you by day,
nor the moon by night.

The LORD will keep you
from all evil;
he will keep your life.
The LORD will keep your going out
and your coming in
from this time on and forevermore. -- Psalm 121 (NRSV)

MY PRAYER LIST

TOPICAL INDEX

SCRIPTURE INDEX

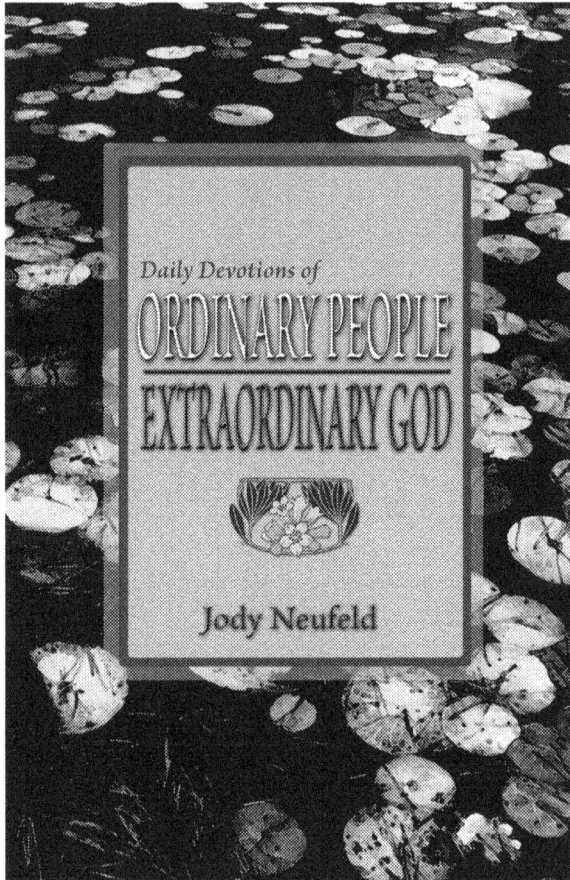

Ideal for prayer and study groups!

Jody Neufeld's daily devotional book, Daily Devotions of Ordinary People – Extraordinary God has become a favorite of many for individual devotional reading. This small, weekly book has 52 devotions along with study and discussion questions for small groups that meet weekly. Call us at (805) 968-1001 or see our web site (http://www.energionpubs.com) for quantity discounts. Suggested Retail: $7.99.

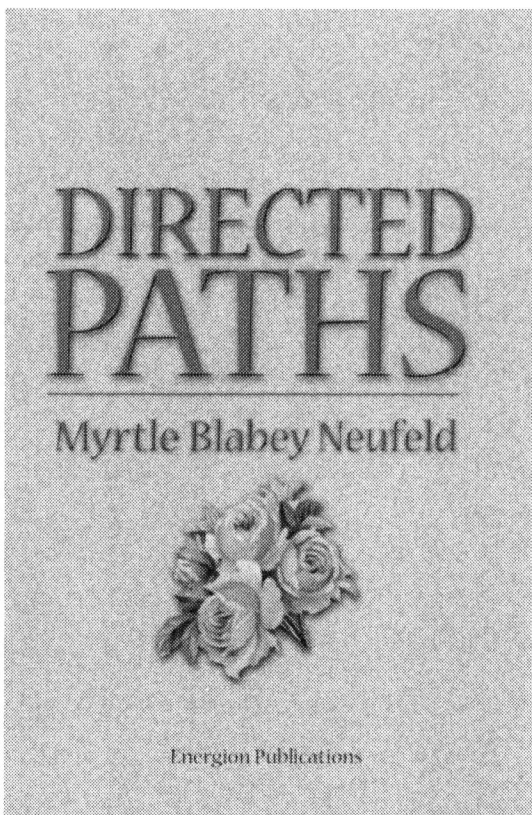

I Want to Pray!

Opening Communication With God

by

Perry M. Dalton

&

Henry E. Neufeld

*2nd Edition
(Revised and Expanded)*

I Want to Pray! provides basic, practical information on prayer and suggestions for study and individual and group activities. Build your prayer life with this helpful guide. Suggested Retail: $7.99. See our web site (http://www.energionpubs.com) or call (850) 968-1001.

IDENTIFYING
YOUR GIFTS AND SERVICE
SMALL GROUP EDITION

THERE ARE DIFFERENT TYPES OF GIFTS,
BUT THE SAME SPIRIT
THERE ARE DIFFERENT TYPES OF SERVICES,
BUT THE SAME LORD
THERE ARE DIFFERENT TYPES OF ACTIVITIES,
BUT THE SAME GOD
WHO WORKS EVERYTHING IN EVERYONE.

1 CORINTHIANS 12: 4 - 6

HENRY E. NEUFELD

This practical guide outlines a Holy Spirit led approach to discovering your spiritual gifts and finding a place to use them in service. It is oriented toward the community, directing each person to work with church leadership in ministry. Suggested Retail: $7.99. See our web site (http://www.energionpubs.com) or call (850) 968-1001.

www.ingramcontent.com/pod-product-compliance
Lightning Source LLC
Chambersburg PA
CBHW031606040426
42452CB00006B/428